Sound Advice on

Digital Audio

by Bill Gibson

Sound Advice on Digital Audio
by Bill Gibson

SVP, Thomson Course Technology PTR: Andy Shafran
Publisher: Stacy L. Hiquet
Executive Editor: Mike Lawson
Senior Marketing Manager: Sarah O'Donnell
Marketing Manager: Heather Hurley
Manager of Editorial Services: Heather Talbot
Associate Marketing Manager: Kristin Eisenzopf
Marketing Coordinator: Jordan Casey
Project Editor: Cathleen D. Snyder
PTR Editorial Services Coordinator: Elizabeth Furbish
Cover Designer: Stephen Ramirez

Special thanks to Mackie.

Educational facilities, companies, and organizations interested in multiple copies or licensing of this book should contact the publisher for quantity discount information. Training manuals, CD-ROMs, and portions of this book are also available individually or can be tailored for specific needs.

ISBN: 1-931140-39-1
Library of Congress Catalog Card Number: 2004115243
Printed in the United States of America
04 05 06 07 08 DR 10 9 8 7 6 5 4 3 2 1

THOMSON
COURSE TECHNOLOGY
Professional ■ Trade ■ Reference

Thomson Course Technology PTR, a division of Thomson Course Technology
25 Thomson Place
Boston, MA 02210
http://www.courseptr.com

Contents

Analog versus Digital

Digital recording is different from analog in that it doesn't operate in a continuous way; it breaks a continuously varying waveform into a sequence of individual amplitude assessments called samples. Digital technology attempts to sample the amplitude enough times per second to accurately recreate th e analog waveform. The result is a stair-step version of an originally continuous wave.

Since a digital recorder is typically only referencing digital data stored on a hard drive or other digital storage medium, its actions are usually nondestructive and undoable, with complete provision to perform computer functions such as cut, copy, and paste. These features provide amazing power and manipulative potential. As we jump into the workings of digital recording, we'll see just how capable this system is of providing creative opportunities for building amazing music.

Analog Wave Compared to Digital Wave

Digital recording breaks a continuously varying waveform into a sequence of individual amplitude assessments called samples. Digital technology attempts to sample the amplitude enough times per second to accurately recreate the analog waveform. The result is a stair-step version of an originally continuous wave. Notice the smooth, continuously varying waveform of the analog waveform and the digitally sampled simulation.

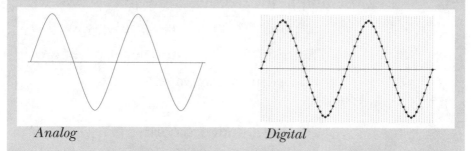

Analog   Digital

Connecting the sample points creates a stair-step version of the analog waveform. The process of changing the analog wave into a digital representation is referred to as analog-to-digital conversion. Conversely, the process of changing the digital picture back into an analog form is called digital-to-analog conversion. The closer the samples are together, the more accurate the digital version of the waveform.

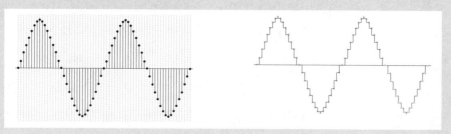

Even with the power offered by digital manipulation of audio data, musical creativity, emotion, passion, and authenticity are essential. No amount of gear can make up for a lack of musical inspiration and talent, but digital tools can help convey the message of a true talent. They propel the creative process, and, if used properly, won't get in the way and slow things down.

Digital Theory Basics

It's important to understand the previous information in order to have a frame of reference to help you build an understanding of digital recording. The digital recording concept is actually simple. An energy-level reading is taken a specified number of times per second, then recorded on a grid. The individual readings together represent a building-block version of the analog waveform.

Imagine that several times per second an energy reading (called a sample) is taken, measuring the amplitude of an analog sound wave. The first reading measures nine units of amplitude. The second reading measures three units. The third, fourth, fifth, and sixth readings register six, nine, 11, and 10 units. These are followed by four more consecutive readings of 11, nine, six, and nine, then negative values for each of the amplitude measurements. If you were to plot these readings on a graph and draw a line connecting each unit, you'd see the analog waveform represented by this set of discrete amplitude readings.

What's So Good about Digital Recording?

Signal-to-Noise Ratio

Both analog and digital recording are ideally transparent—they should represent the real sound faithfully and accurately. Excellent analog recording gear does an amazing job of capturing the depth and warmth of sound. However, tape noise can be a problem. Some digital recordings offer 144-dB S/N ratio, better than double that of many analog recorders.

The process of digital recording itself allows for very little noise, unless it comes from the source.

Accurate Copies

Digital recording offers the potential for a system where the copy is as good as the original—an unlikely possibility in the analog domain. Although the accuracy of the digital clone is suspect, the possibility is still a theoretical reality. A clone is an exact, number-for-number copy of the digital data. Clones are more accurate and dependable when the file stays in the hard disk domain. Copies that go to and from DAT and CD recorders and other such devices are subject to an error correction scheme, therefore running a high risk of transferring with several inaccuracies in hard data.

Media

Digital data can be stored on any media common to computer data storage. A file created on a hard-disk recording system can be saved, archived, and played back from several common data storage platforms: magnetic disk, CD, cartridges, or other optical formats. Fast access time is required for playback of digital audio, but the speed requirements are met by most data storage systems.

Storage Cost

The cost of storage for digital audio is much less expensive than storage of analog audio. A reel of 2-inch tape—commonly used for 24-track analog recording—might hold 16 minutes of music and cost $175.00. In comparison, an entire album of digital audio can typically be archived on 10 to 15 CDs at a total cost of around $10.00. Data storage is reliable and accurate. In addition, as technology and storage media change, the data can be easily transferred for future use and long-term archiving.

Editing Capabilities

In the digital domain, the audio becomes data and can be manipulated like any other data. Cut, copy, paste, crossfade, level changes, and undo are common actions. Editing is a dream; the possibilities are boundless.

Speed

Digital systems offer an amazing advantage in transport speed. Computer-based systems have no rewind time. Location of musical sections is simple and instantaneous. There is always instant availability of any musical section, track, or instrument. The days of rewinding back and forth through a reel of analog tape are fading. Though some engineers still prefer the sound of analog tape and are willing to withstand its pitfalls, working in the disk-based digital domain is far more efficient and hassle free—as long as your computer doesn't crash.

Bits/Bytes/Words

Bit

A bit is an individual integer used as part of a group. In my American Heritage Dictionary, a bit is defined as:

1. A single character of a language having just two characters, as either of the binary digits 0 or 1.
2. A unit of information equivalent to the choice of either of two equally likely alternatives.
3. A unit of information storage capacity.
4. A contraction of "binary" and "digit." B(INARY) + (DIG)IT

Word

A word is simply a multidigit binary number made up of bits. The number of bits in a word represents the smallest unit of addressable memory in a microprocessor environment (a computer). The number of bits in a word is called its word length.

Byte

An 8-bit word is called a byte. The term byte comes from the contraction of "by eight," which was derived from the concept of a bit multiplied by eight.

The digit on the left-hand side of the word is called the most significant bit (MSB). The digit on the right-hand side of the word is called the least significant bit (LSB).

Advantage of Binary Code/PCM

A binary code represents the least possible number of digits for the processing environment, where each representation is compiled of a series of 1s and 0s. Anything that's not 0 is 1. This creates a scenario where there's no question as to the numeric value of a digital code. In digital recording, each value of the sampled waveform is represented by a series of 0s and 1s. Noise on the media is inconsequential, unlike on analog tape. In the digital domain, noise on the actual media or a slight hazing of the data has no real effect on the actual waveform represented. If the D/A converter is sent a 1 in any form, it's registered as a 1. If it's sent a lack of 1, it's registered as a 0.

With only two possible values, methods for encoding and decoding the data flow are simplified. The most common form of digital encoding is Pulse Code Modulation (PCM), where a 1 is represented by the existence of the pulse (pulse on) and 0 is represented by the lack of a pulse (pulse off). With this simple system and a synchronous clock that controls the pulse rate, it's an elementary matter to read, store, and play back the data.

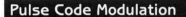

Pulse Code Modulation is a very common means of transmitting digital data. Binary data flow is indicated by a stream of on and off pulses. A pulse indicates the integer 1, while the lack of a pulse indicates a 0. On the sample grid, each of the sample points has a discrete number of possible amplitude steps.

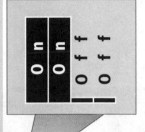

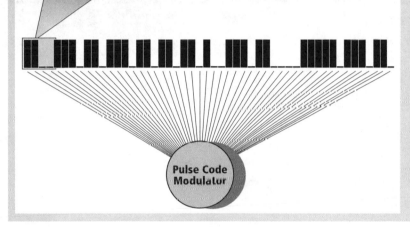

Pulse Code
Modulator

Samples

Rate

The process of sampling (digital encoding and decoding) breaks the time axis (horizontal) and the voltage axis (vertical) into a specific number of discrete steps.

At each step along the time axis, a measurement is taken of voltage (amplitude) status. This process, called sampling, results in a stair-step picture of the analog waveform.

Sampling

At each time interval, the amplitude is quantified according to the discrete steps available. The number of amplitude steps available is determined by the word size. An 8-bit word allows for 256 discrete steps from amplitude off to peak amplitude. A 16-bit word provides 65,536 amplitude units.

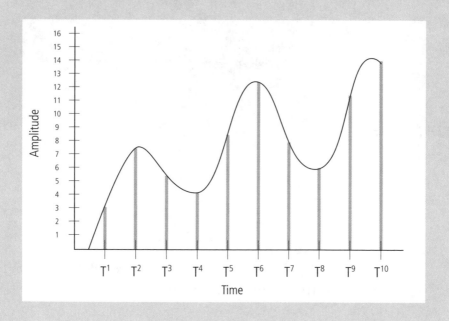

The number of times per second the processor samples the voltage (amplitude) of the analog waveform is called the sample rate. The more times the processor samples the analog status of the waveform, the greater the potential accuracy of the system. According to the Nyquist Theorem, the sample rate must be at least twice the highest desired frequency. Therefore, to accurately and faithfully capture a bandwidth extending up to 20 kHz (the upper range of human hearing), the sample rate must be at least 40 kHz (2 x 20 kHz). In order to ensure accuracy and to provide headroom for the system, the standard audio CD sample rate was fixed at 44.1 kHz.

Controversy follows the question of whether there is a need for higher sample rates and longer word length. Some felt originally that a 44.1-kHz 16-bit sample was sufficient, since filters effectively eliminate artifacts above 20 kHz, and 20 kHz is the upper limit of mankind's hearing range. However, since all frequencies interact acoustically and work together to create a waveform, it seems believable and practical that capturing a broader frequency range and a more accurate resolution is necessary.

Localization

The concern regarding sample rate isn't simply frequency-related. Since no one, not even the newest-born baby, can hear above 25 or 26 kHz anyway, the implied ideal sample rate might be 50 to 55 kHz. However, there's more involved in our hearing and perception than frequency. Much of our perception comes from our stereo perception of localization and positioning on a three-dimensional plane. The messages that our brain responds to are based on a triangulation process involving both ears and the sound source. The brain calculates the time delay difference between the arrival of a sound at either ear. The time and EQ variations, as a sound moves around the head, are translated into left-right and front-back positioning cues. As the high frequencies are affected by the physical part of the outer ear, called the pinna, changes of equalization cue the brain about front-to-back positioning. Perception of left-right positioning is a product of the brain's interpretation of timing differences between the arrival time of a sound at each ear. All things considered, the human hearing and localization systems are amazingly complex and efficient.

It's been determined that time delay differences of 15 microseconds between left and right ears are easily discernible by nearly anyone. That's less than the time difference between two samples at 48 kHz (about 20 microseconds). Using a single pulse, one microsecond in length as a source, some listeners can perceive time delay differences of as little as five microseconds between left and right. It is therefore indicated that in order to provide a system with exact accuracy concerning imaging and positioning, the individual samples should be less than five microseconds apart. At 96 kHz (an often preferred sample rate), there is a 10.417-microsecond space between samples. At a 192-kHz sample rate, there is a 5.208-microsecond space between samples, suggesting that a sample rate of

The Ultimate Sample Rate

Sample A represents a 48-kHz sample. The time distance between individual samples, at this rate, is about 20 microseconds (20 millionths of a second). Since many listeners can perceive time delays of as little as five microseconds between the left and right channels, it seems obvious that a 48-kHz sample rate is incapable of providing the localization accuracy necessary to guarantee perfectly faithful imaging.

Sample B represents a 192-kHz sample. The samples are just over five microseconds apart.

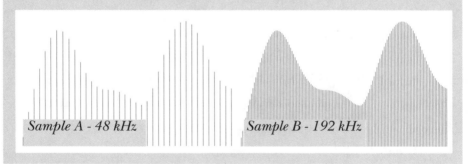

Sample A - 48 kHz   Sample B - 192 kHz

192 kHz is optimal. As processors increase in speed and efficiency and as storage capacity expands high sample rates, long word lengths will become an insignificant concern, and we'll be able to focus on the next audio catastrophe. Maybe full integration of tactile virtual audio and video imagery.

Quantization/Bits

At each sample point, signal strength (amplitude) is calculated. Amplitude, in an analog domain, is continuously variable. In the digital domain, amplitude is measured against a grid of discrete stair steps. The resolution of the stair steps is determined by the binary word length. An 8-bit word offers 256 discrete levels with which to define the momentary amplitude. The more bits in the word, the finer the resolution. A word with more bits can more accurately define the amplitude at each sample point.

At first guess, most of us assume that a 16-bit word offers twice the resolution of an 8-bit word: 512 discrete steps. That is definitely not the case. In reality, each additional bit adds a significant amount of resolution because the increase is calculated exponentially, not through simple addition. If we consider a 1-bit word, there are really only two options: digit on (1) or digit off (0). With this in mind, the number 2 becomes our constant, and the number of bits (n) becomes our exponent, expressed as 2^n—verbally expressed as "2 to the nth power." It simply means two times itself n number of times. The number of discrete steps of resolution available to indicate specific amplitude at any given sample point is easily calculated. If you have an n-bit word, where n represents the number of bits, calculate 2 times itself, n number of times. For example, in an 8-bit word n = 8, so the resolution is expressed as 28, or 2 x 2 x 2 x 2 x 2 x 2 x 2 x 2, or 256.

A 1-bit word is mathematically calculated as two to the first power (2^1). A 2-bit word offers four steps (2^2 or 2 x 2) to calculate amplitude (11, 10, 01, 00). It's easy for us to see all the options when we have small word sizes, but it's also easy to get confused regarding the big picture, so let's continue with our examples. A 3-bit word offers eight steps (2^3 or 2 x 2 x 2) of resolution to calculate sample point amplitude: 000, 001, 010, 011, 111, 110, 100, 101. A 4-bit word provides 16 discrete steps (2^4 or 2 x 2 x 2 x 2). As the bits increase, the resolution dramatically increases. Notice that each additional bit doubles the resolution; that's the power of the binary system. A change from 16 bits to 18 bits is a full four times greater (400 percent) in resolution; if you calculated incorrectly, you might think there was only a 12.5 percent increase in resolution. The number of steps available to define each sample amplitude in a 16-bit word is calculated as 2^{16}, which equals 65,536 steps. In comparison, a 24-bit word provides a resolution of 16,777,216 steps per sample point!

Aliasing

When a digital recorder attempts to sample a frequency higher than half the sample rate, the sampling process produces inaccurate and randomly inconsistent waveform characteristics. These high frequencies, called aliasing frequencies, must be filtered out before they arrive at the A/D converter.

When the audio source bandwidth is properly filtered, using a high-quality low-pass filter, the sample is accurate and clean. When audio source bandwidth is improperly filtered, sometimes the resulting sound is inconsistent with probable random artifacts in the lower frequencies. Since low-pass filters cut a bandwidth according to a slope rather than a hard and fast frequency cutoff, sample rates for full bandwidth sound sources are set at about

10 percent higher than twice the highest recorded frequency. This provides processing headroom, assuring the recordist of the best possible sound quality.

RAM Buffer

Data flow playback rate is important. Since minor distortions, or noise, included in the storage media exhibit the potential to create jitter and other timing anomalies, a system is necessary to stabilize and guarantee accurate and consistent data flow. Digital data, audio in particular, is referenced to a stable, centralized timing clock (word clock) that controls the transmission and conversion of each sample. Samples are played back at a rate controlled by the word clock. In a 16-bit system, the computer progresses through the 16-bit words at the master clock rate. Therefore, data recorded at 48 kHz can be played back in reference to a 44.1-kHz clock (or any other word clock speed), but its pitch and speed will adjust relative to the playback sample rate.

As an assurance that the playback rate will remain constant and stable, the processor stores up a certain amount of data as a backup—a buffer. This buffer protects the system from prematurely

The Ram Buffer

Data flows into the RAM buffer at a rate determined by its needs. If the buffer begins to fill up, the data slows down to compensate. If the buffer begins to empty out, the data flow increases. Once in the buffer, the data is released at a constant rate, determined by the word clock. In this way, there's a rock-solid, steady flow of digital data, even if the data flow is momentarily interrupted due to errors or other anomalies.

CD Player, Digital Machine, DVD, etc.

DIGITAL DATA STREAM 11000111 00011110

RAM BUFFER

DIGITAL DATA OUTPUT CLOCKED PERFECTLY 01100 101010100

The steady, constant data clock can only let data exit the RAM buffer at the selected sample rate.

running out of data. Data flows from the buffer in direct sync with the master timing clock. The tape speed or disc access is determined by the needs of the RAM buffer. If data is emptying out of the RAM buffer, the tape speeds up to fill it in, or the disc picks up the pace to keep up with the data flow. There is no pitch variation, since the RAM buffer outputs the data at an extremely constant rate, which is either determined by the internal word clock, an external sync source, or by the word clock of the master device.

Sample Rate Options

The number of times a processor samples a waveform is often definable by the user. Nevertheless, standard sample rates apply to specific applications. Most of the following sample rates are common in the digital audio industry.

44.1 kHz

The standard sample rate for an audio compact disc is 44,100 times per second (also referred to as 44.1 kHz, or 44.1 k). At this sample rate, it's possible to get an accurate replica of an analog waveform.

48 kHz

Another common sample rate is 48 kHz. It was originally held as more of a semi-professional sample rate, until recordists began to see that even the small increase in sample rate from 44.1 k to 48 k made a noticeable difference in the sound quality. Many very high-quality recordings have been mixed to 48-kHz sample rates, then mastered through an analog process to the digital compact disc format. In fact, 48-kHz sampling quickly became the preferred professional format whenever the project didn't require direct transfer to CD. When developing audio for direct transfer to CD, many engineers prefer to work in the lesser format (44.1 kHz) rather than second-guess the effect of digital format conversion.

32 kHz

The broadcast standard is 32 kHz. Most radio broadcasts are operated within the limitations of a 15-kHz bandwidth, so a sample rate of 32 kHz is a perfect fit. The slower sample rate utilizes about 27.44 percent less storage space, letting radio stations put more programming on each medium. Considering radio's limited bandwidth, there would be no practical benefit to broadcasting at 44.1, 48, or even 96 kHz. Any radio show or other program being simultaneously broadcast over airwaves and full-bandwidth cable could only optimize their sound quality by transmitting at the full-bandwidth frequency du jour.

44.056 kHz

This is the original Sony PCM-F1 sample rate.

22.050 and 11.125 kHz

These lower-fidelity sample rates are used primarily in computer-specific documents (Macintosh or PC). The primary purpose of this sample rate is limiting file size for use in programming or for data transmission in low baud rate Internet connections.

11.125 kHz

This is a low-fidelity sample rate used primarily in computer-specific documents. Like the 22.5-kHz sample rate, the primary purpose in considering this sample rate is limiting file size for use in programming or for data transmission in low baud rate Internet connections.

22.254 and 11.127 kHz

These low-fidelity sample rates are used for playback on older Macintosh computers that don't support 16-bit audio playback.

96 kHz

Samples performed at 96 kHz are typically based on a 24-bit word. They provide amazing capability for precise digital interpretation of the broadest-bandwidth audio source. A 16-bit, 44.1-kHz sample provides for 2,890,137,600 possible options (grid points) per second to define the analog waveform. On the other hand, consider that a 96-kHz, 24-bit waveform supplies a grid of 1,610,612,736,000 possible points per second with which to define the wave. It seems obvious that the 24-bit, 96-kHz sample is great way to go—if you have enough room to store all the data.

192 kHz

Some feel this is the optimum sample rate, primarily because it offers sufficient resolution for precise localization information.

Listen to the following audio examples, comparing the sonic character of a few different sample rates. Each example was recorded into its particular format, then rerecorded through the analog outs into a digital editing workstation, to capture as much of the personality of each sample rate as possible.

Audio Example 1

44.1 kHz

Audio Example 2

48 kHz

Audio Example 3

32 kHz

Audio Example 4

22.050 kHz

Audio Example 5

11.025 kHz

Dither/Quantization Error

At especially low signal levels, the digital recording system performs very poorly. In a 16-bit system, a low-level signal, around 10 percent of maximum level, uses just under two bits to record whatever audio signal is present. These low-level signals are common during the fadeout of a commercial song and during classical recordings: symphony, choir, string quartet, etc.

Listen to Audio Examples 6 through 8 for a demonstration of the digital recording system's efficiency at these low levels.

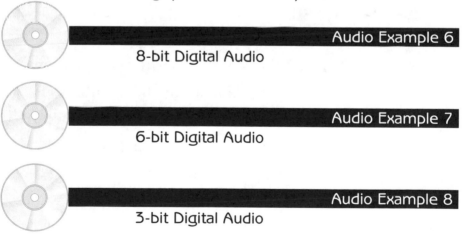

Audio Example 6
8-bit Digital Audio

Audio Example 7
6-bit Digital Audio

Audio Example 8
3-bit Digital Audio

Dither is simply white noise added to the program source at very low levels (typically half the least significant bit). Though it seems ironic to add noise to an otherwise noiseless system, the inaccuracies and waveform distortions of these low-level signals must be addressed.

Dithering provides a means to more accurate recording at low levels. Noise combines with the signal in a way that increases the overall amplitude, therefore realizing greater accuracy through increased bits. In fact, dither enables the encoding of amplitudes smaller than the LSB.

Dither combines with the outgoing digital signal in a way that combines for linearity of audio playback. Although it uses noise as an active part of the process, dithering is worthwhile, considering the improvement it gives us in accuracy and linearity.

Dither is typically selected as a function at the input to the A/D converter or on its output. The correlation between error and signal can be removed through the addition of dither prior to the A/D converter. Therefore, the effects of quantization error are randomized. Dither

Dither

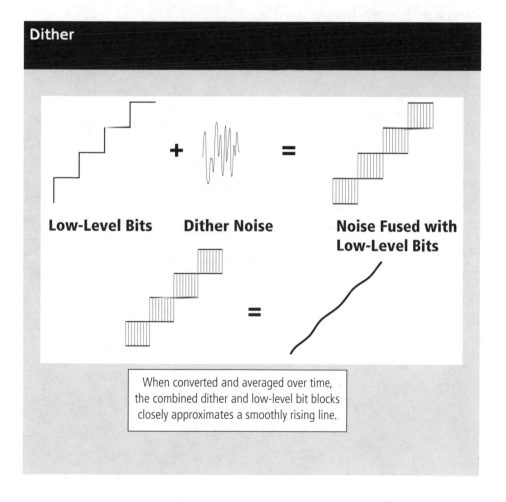

Low-Level Bits   **Dither Noise**   **Noise Fused with Low-Level Bits**

When converted and averaged over time, the combined dither and low-level bit blocks closely approximates a smoothly rising line.

doesn't simply mask the artifacts; it removes them.

Dithering is typically left for the final stage of production. A recordist should rely on the mastering stage of a project to reap the advantages of dithering.

Noise Shaping

Noise shaping is a part of the dithering process. It helps shift the dither noise into a less audible frequency range to provide the best results with the least audible noise. Digital filters move the dither noise out of the ear's most sensitive frequency range (about 4 kHz) and into a less noticeable range. Noise shaping is not a necessary part of the dithering process, but it helps optimize the process through decreased audible noise.

Two types of noise shaping commonly occur in the mastering process:

- First-Order Noise Shaping – White noise is optimized for dithering by including a first-order high-pass response that rolls off at 6 dB/octave below 15 kHz.
- Second-Order Noise Shaping – White noise is optimized for dithering by including a second-order high-pass response that rolls off at 12 dB/octave below 20 kHz. This scheme also includes a dip in response at 4 kHz, where the ear is most sensitive. The actual amount of noise induced by second-order noise shaping is greater than in first-order shaping. However, second-order shaping results in noise that's less audible.

Converters

Sound originates naturally in an analog manner. The waveform created by any acoustic sound source is analog in that it consists of continuously varying amplitude. The device that calculates the digital equivalent of the analog waveform is called the analog-to-digital (A/D) converter. It samples at the proper rate, and it performs all the functions necessary to ensure accurate and dependable transfer of amplitude variations into a continuous binary data flow. The importance of the converter quality is paramount to successful and satisfactory digital recording.

The digital-to-analog (D/A) converter receives the digital data flow at its input and converts the digital information into an analog voltage. Ideally, a signal that starts acoustically and is then converted to digital data will match its analog source once its converted from data back to acoustic analog voltage.

A/D and D/A conversion are very complex. The conversion process must happen in sync with the storage media, the quantization rate must be stable and controlled, and the converter must be capable of accurately handling the bulk of data involved in high-quality digital audio.

The math involved in this conversion is impressive. The speed with which the data must be processed is overwhelming. The accuracy and clarity of digital recording is amazing. Sampling and quantization are performed by the A/D converter. The D/A converter simply plots the quantized samples back into a continuously varying analog form.

Oversampling

The purpose of oversampling is to increase the accuracy of the conversion system. The actual process creates a conversion that allows for a gently sloped and less intrusive anti-aliasing filter. Traditional sample recording and playback call for an extreme "brick wall" filter at the Nyquist Frequency (half the sample rate). A less extreme filter causes less phase error and results in a cleaner, smoother digital conversion.

The oversampling process is ingenious, requiring a processor capable of high sample rates. Typical oversample systems operate at between two and 128 times the regular sample rate. As an example, at eight times oversampling, seven artificial samples are created between the actual samples, all at zero level. Now there are eight samples in the place of the original one, increasing the sample rate by a factor of eight. A 44.1 kHz sample rate would, therefore, be increased to 352.8 kHz. The seven blank (zero-level) samples are interpolated by the processor. In other words, it guesses what their values would be according to the status of the original samples.

Oversampling typically occurs at both ends of the digital data flow. Incoming analog waveforms are oversampled into the A/D converter, providing all the

Graph A exhibits the original sample amplitudes of a digital recording that hasn't been oversampled. The analog waveform is indicated accurately but an extreme filter would be necessary to ensure that there are no aliasing problems.

Graph B exhibits an eight times oversample of the waveform represented by Graph A. The gray sample amplitudes (S1, S2, S3, etc.) represent the original samples. The black amplitudes between the gray ones represent the processor-generated and interpolated oversamples. In oversampling, the processor creates several zero-level samples between the originals. The processor then interpolates (guesses) at what the values of the oversamples should be and adjusts their amplitudes appropriately.

Digital audio that has been oversampled is much less prone to aliasing problems.

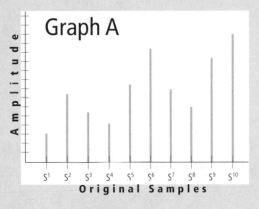

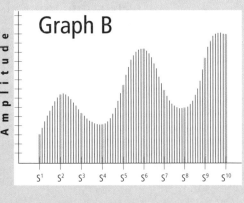

benefits of the oversampling process. For data storage, a circuit called a decimator reverts the high sample rate to the Nyquist rate (44.1 kHz in the case of the standard CD). On playback, the digital data is again oversampled by passing through a digital filter called an interpolator. This process allows for the best of both worlds, since the data is efficiently and accurately converted, recorded, and played back. In addition, data storage is at the Nyquist rate rather than the increased rate, providing concise storage and premium audio quality.

Dynamic Range

Dynamic range is the distance, measured in decibels, between the loudest and quietest audible sounds in an audio system or component. The dynamic range of any digital recording system is roughly six times the number of bits. The dynamic range of a 16-bit system is about 96 dB; the dynamic range of a 24-bit system is about 144 dB.

Format Conversion

Digital format conversion is common and involves converting from one sample rate to another as well as between basic languages (S/P DIF, AES/EBU, TDIF, etc.). The simplest conversions utilize unchanged data with variations in ID codes. Complex format conversions relate sample rates and word length in a mathematical manner. Then it's up to the processor to calculate the comparison.

Format conversions can take quite a while to perform because of the bulk of calculated data. A processor converting a 24-bit 48-kHz sample to a 16-bit 32-kHz sample must recalculate the sample positions of the new format in relation to the old. Not only does the processor have to calculate the new format data, it also has to interpret the original data and translate it to a form that can then be interpreted. As processor speeds and data transmission rates increase, format conversion will become more accurate and tolerable.

Many software- and hardware-based systems perform real-time format conversion. The accuracy of these systems depends on processor speed and accuracy as well as the integrity of the mathematical conversion. The content of the material being converted also determines the sonic stability. In other words, sometimes it sounds good and sometimes it doesn't.

Errors

It's not practical to expect error-free digital recordings. There's always a chance of imperfections in the media or momentary noise interference in the flow of data. An environment with an ideal signal-to-noise ratio doesn't eliminate the chance of errors. Although it might minimize the chance of errors, it offers no guarantee that they won't happen. Error-correction schemes offer a way to overcome error problems, often in a way that restores the data to its original form. However, certain repairs are merely approximations of the original data. These schemes explain the change in audio quality associated with multiple digital copies, especially in the sequential digital recording media, such as DAT.

In the digital domain, two types of data errors occur frequently: bit errors and burst errors. Occasional noise impulses cause bit inaccuracies. These bit errors are more or less audible, depending on where the error occurs within the word. Errors in the least significant bit (LSB) will probably be masked, especially in louder passages. On the other hand, errors in the most significant bit (MSB) can cause loud and irritating transient clicks or pops.

Tape dropouts or other media imperfections, such as scratches on a disk, can cause errors in digital data flow called burst errors. Burst errors, like bit errors, are potentially devastating to conversion of data to audio, especially considering that they represent larger areas of data confusion.

Data Protection

Given that errors are certain to occur, a system called interleaving is commonly used to minimize the risk of losing large amounts of data. Interleaving data is similar in concept to diversifying investments. If you spread your money between several investments, there's little chance you'll lose it all. Similarly, interleaving spreads the digital word out over a noncontiguous section of storage media. That way, if a bit or burst error corrupts data, it probably won't corrupt an entire word or group of words. The damage will only affect part of the word, and the likelihood is great that correction schemes will sufficiently repair any losses.

Interleaving

The interleaving scheme inputs the samples into a grid in numerical order. Once in the grid, they're then sent out in a way that redistributes the sample order. Whereas the samples enter the grid in rows, they exit the grid in columns. Since sequentially consecutive samples are physically separated during storage, any disk-related errors probably won't catastrophically damage audio quality. It is, however, imperative that the samples are put back into their correct order before playback.

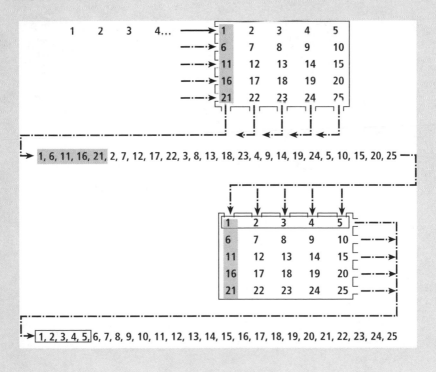

Interleaving happens at both ends of the digital recording process. From A/D, converter data is interleaved as it stores on the medium. Just before the data is returned to an analog form, the interleaved data is reconstructed to its original form. This clever scheme provides a system that is completely faithful to the original data, while spreading the risk of damaged or lost data.

Error Detection

Most error-correction schemes utilize a form of a code word to indicate the existence of an error and to indicate the possible actions necessary for correction. A code word is made up of additional bits added to each digital word. These bits typically indicate certain traits of the digital word. They're used as a means to verify the integrity of data storage and transfer.

Parity is the most basic form of error detection. The parity system simply adds one bit, called the "parity bit," to each word and attaches a meaning to its status. If there are an even number of 1s in a word, the parity bit status is set to 1. If there's an odd number of 1s in a word, the parity bit is set to 0. Once the parity bits have been set in the recording process, they can be checked in the playback process. Parity is checked on each word during conversion to analog. If a bit has been damaged, causing a discrepancy in the relationship between the odd-even status of the word and the parity bit, the word is identified as being in error. This is a simple system and introduces an important concept to error detection, though it begins to fail any time more than one of the bits has been damaged. In addition, it offers no means of identifying which bit has been damaged.

There are more elaborate code word systems based on the principle of parity that are more suited to the complex task of faithfully correcting audio data. They extend the concept to include additional

The parity system simply adds one bit, called the "parity bit," to each word. If there are an even number of 1s in a word, the parity bit status is set to 1. If there's an odd number of 1s in a word, the parity bit is set to 0. Whereas, the parity bits are set in the record process, they're checked on each word during playback and conversion to analog. For example, if a word has been tagged for even parity (an even number of 1s) then on playback an odd number of 1s is detected, the word is recognized to be in error. A word recognized in error will be bypassed.

DATA	Parity Bit	Error Status
1100 0011 0110 0011	1	OK
1100 0011 0110 0011	0	error
0110 0000 1111 0100	0	OK
1010 0100 1000 0001	1	error
0001 0011 0010 0111	0	OK
1100 0011 0110 0011	1	OK

bits in a complex mathematical relationship to create parity words out of blocks of data. Cyclic Redundancy Check Code (CRCC), Reed-Solomon Codes, Hamming Codes, and Convolutional Codes are examples of these.

Error Correction

The beauty of the binary system is that data is either correct or incorrect. There's no coloration or subjective influence as there is in the analog domain. If the data is incorrect and it can be identified, there's only one step to correcting it—change the incorrect 1 to a 0, or vice versa. The trick is finding the error, not correcting it.

There are two basic principles behind error correction: redundancy and concealment. Within these systems, several error-correction schemes might be put into action.

Redundancy

True redundancy involves storing the same data in two or more separate areas on the medium, then comparing and reconstructing the data based on those comparisons. If one word contains an error and it can be determined as such, the redundant word or words can be used to verify and restore the data to its original state. The problems with a simple redundancy system lie in the dramatically increased storage capacity and processing speed requirements. Therefore, clever schemes have been developed that add bits to each word to assist in the detection of any questionable data. Though these systems might or might not be successful all the time, they offer partial correction, at the very least. Remaining errors can be handled through concealment or muting.

Concealment
If data is lost altogether and cannot be reconstructed through a redundancy system, it can be reconstructed through an educated guess on the part of the processor. If a word is missing or corrupt, this scheme simply looks at the word before and after the error, then calculates the average of the two and places it in the gap. This process of mathematical guesswork is called interpolation. Though it doesn't guarantee the exact replacement of the

lost data, it typically provides a reasonable facsimile in which the difference is usually inaudible.

Muting

There is also a protection system in place in case error correction fails. In the case of gross errors, the system simply mutes the particular word or words in question. This is typically an infrequent occurrence and, as such, it is inaudible in most cases.

Storage Media

Once we enter the digital arena, our music, no matter how artistically inspired or created, becomes data. The simple beauty surrounding this concept lies in the inherent ability to store, restore, copy, paste, encode, and decode this data with, theoretically, no degradation. Once a musical piece is transformed into digital data, there's little significance as to its storage format. As long as the medium is capable of reading and writing quickly enough to avoid a data bottleneck, the data should be stored and retrieved accurately. The primary consideration is the data storage protocol. Does the medium use an error-correction scheme, or does it simply transfer the binary file bit by bit?

Backing Up

Be sure to take the time to regularly back up all data files. If you've had a particularly rough day in the studio, that's a great reason to back up all your files—who wants to relive a bad day?

Storage media have become so inexpensive that there's no real excuse not to back up. When I'm in the middle of an intense recording time, I back up at the end of each day. Anything that has been changed is backed up. Sometimes, if a file is so huge that it won't easily fit on the backup format I happen to be using, I'll simply copy the entire file to another place on my hard drive. This is a quick process, and I can simply set it to copy and leave.

In the modern world of recording, large drives are inexpensive, and a good DVD drive can save the day. Regular back-ups can save the day—and the project.

CD—Compact Disc

The standard compact disc holds 650 megabytes of audio, video, or computer data. This medium revolutionized the public perceptions and expectations regarding the audio world. Sound without scratches, pops, clicks, and hisses was easy to get used to. As a storage medium, they offer an inexpensive option to the high-priced portable hard-drive formats.

A CD holds 74 minutes of stereo sound at a sample rate of 44.1 kHz with a 16-bit word length.

The CD recording process uses a 4 3/4-inch reflective disk to store data. The data writer creates tiny bumps on the disk surface that correlate to the binary bits. The read head shines an intense beam of light at the disk surface, perceiving each bump through the change in light reflection caused by the bumps themselves. In the absence of a bump, the light is reflected directly to a sensor. The presence of any bump or pit interrupts that reflection, instantly signaling a change in status of digital data. The concept is simple when you know that the presence or absence of a bump on the disk surface merely indicates a variation between 1 and 0. What is mind boggling is the speed at which these changes are recognized.

HD-CD

A high-density compact disc (HD-CD) operates on exactly the same principle as a standard CD—the difference lies in how large and closely grouped the bumps are. An 8x HD-CD has eight times as many bumps in the same amount of space as a standard CD. These bumps are also eight times smaller than on a standard CD; therefore, the beam of light required to read the high-density disc must be at least eight times smaller than a standard CD reader.

CD-R and CD-RW

CD-R discs can only be recorded once, but they can be read any number of times. The early versions of this concept were called WORM drives (Write Once-Read Many). Rewriteable CDs can be reused just like a floppy disk or a regular hard drive. Though the CD-RW discs cost much more than the CD-R discs, they can be cost effective when you know you'll be continually updating data, as is the case with regular data backup.

Like a CD, a CD-R or CD-RW is non-specific as to the type of data stored on it.

DAT

The digital audio tape recorder (DAT) was an instant hit in the recording community. It was really the first digital recorder to become universally accepted and used in the recording industry. Before DAT, Sony offered the F-1 processor, which required setup in conjunction with a videotape recorder, but it didn't come on with the same fire as DAT.

DAT tapes are small, storing up to two hours of full-bandwidth 16-bit PCM stereo audio. The transport mechanism offers fast rewind and fast forward speed, and the machines typically allow for multiple sample rates (32, 44.1, and 48 kHz). Keep in mind that the number of minutes available on each tape increases in direct proportion to the decrease in sample rate. Therefore, you can record more minutes of audio on a DAT tape at 32 kHz than you can at 44.1 kHz.

The DAT recording process that has survived is technically called R-DAT, for Rotating-Head Digital Audio Tape Recorder. This system operates much like a standard videotape recorder. The rotating head helical scan path increases the overall head-to-tape contact speed so that the amount of data required to record high-quality digital audio will fit onto a tape moving at slow speeds.

MiniDisc

This digital format, like CD, holds up to 74 minutes of full-bandwidth stereo audio. Though it accepts the same 16-bit audio source as a CD, it utilizes a data compression scheme called Adaptive Transform Acoustic Coding (ATRAC). This compression architecture essentially eliminates the inaudible part of each word. It relies on the fact that any resultant artifacts or audio inconsistencies will probably be masked by the remaining sound, and that the compressed material might be below the hearing threshold of the human ear.

The audio data is stored in a RAM buffer before it is sent through the D/A converter. This RAM buffer holds up to about ten seconds of data (about a

Digital audio tape recorders (DAT), videotape-based recording systems, and most modular digital multitracks utilize a video-recorder-style transport. Tape is moved, at a relatively slow rate, past a rotating record/playback head. Although the head rotates in the same direction as the tape, it rotates at about 2000 rpm, dramatically increasing the amount of tape-to-head contact speed and time. It's this process which provides the bandwidth necessary to store high-quality, high-density digital audio.

In addition to digital audio tracks, these systems typically provide one or two analog tracks along with a control track for device synchronization.

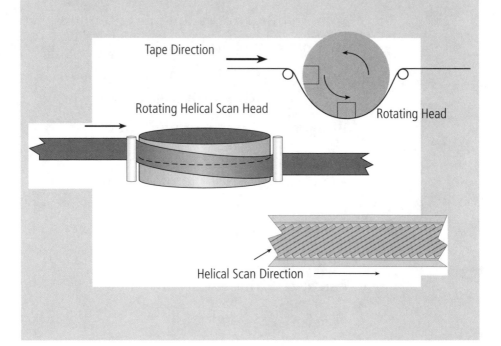

Tape Direction

Rotating Helical Scan Head

Rotating Head

Helical Scan Direction

megabyte). If the player is interrupted by jostling, bumping, or thumping, the flow of the audio out of the buffer won't be interrupted as long as the disruption has ended before the RAM buffer has emptied. Once the disruption ceases, the data simply fills the buffer back up.

Technically, the MiniDisc is a rewriteable magneto-optical disc that uses a laser to apply focused heat to encode the binary bit stream. The actual heat from the laser randomizes and rewrites over previously recorded data.

Hard Drive

The typical hard drive is much like a standard CD in that it writes and reads data from a reflective, spinning disk. Unlike a traditional analog tape recorder, the hard drive doesn't have to write data to the disk in a continuous segment. Depending on the condition, capacity, or fullness of the drive, the data for one song might be written to several noncontiguous (noncontinuous) locations on the drive. Since a hard drive's read/write head moves incredibly fast (faster than the eye can see), data can be accessed randomly from any one point to any other on the disk. When the disk spins fast enough and the read/write moves accurately enough, there's rarely a problem with the continuation of the flow of digital data.

DVD

DVD (Digital Video Disc) is an optical storage medium similar to the compact disc and its variations (CD, CD-ROM, CD-RW). It uses a shorter wavelength that is capable of reading and writing smaller pits on its reflective surface, and it is a two-sided medium that uses multiple layers. The laser can focus on one layer and ignore the other, much in the same way the human eye focuses on a close object while blurring out a distant one. The top layer is partially transmissive, so the laser can focus on it or go through it to the bottom layer.

The DVD is the same physical size as a CD (1.2mm thick and 120 mm in diameter) and the technologies are similar enough that a DVD player can play back a compact disc.

Whereas the CD holds up to 650 MB of data, the DVD holds up to 17 GB. A single-sided, single-layer DVD holds about 4.7 GB; a double-layer DVD holds almost twice that amount (8.5 GB); a double-sided, single layer DVD holds 9.4 GB; and a double-sided, double-layer DVD can hold up to 17 GB. The double-layering method is called Reverse Spiral Dual Layer (RSDL).

Video is stored on the DVD in the Moving Picture Expert Group's MPEG-2 format, while home entertainment audio is stored in a compressed format using Dolby's AC-3 standard, which provides for the 5.1-channel surround sound standard.

Depending on compression schemes, one single-sided, single-layer (4.7-GB) DVD has enough room to hold:

- Two hours and 13 minutes of compressed video at 30 frames per second and 720 x 480 resolution
- Three multichannel audio tracks with 5.1 surround on each track
- Four text tracks for multilanguage subtitles

Optional flags, placed on specific segments, let the studios encode the disc to play R-rated, PG-13, G-rated, or uncensored versions of the same movie. This system provides parents the flexibility to assign maximum age ratings to their children's access codes.

The DVD specification supports access rates of 60 KBps to 1.3 MBps. There are five primary forms of the DVD protocol:

- DVD-ROM is a high-capacity storage medium similar to CD-ROM.

- DVD-Video is designed specifically to hold motion picture content.
- DVD-Audio is similar to an audio CD, designed specifically to hold audio.
- DVD-R permits one-time recordability, with multiple read capability. This acts as data storage space, indiscriminate of format (audio, video, and data).
- DVD-RAM is erasable and rewriteable and, like DVD-R, nonspecific as to content.

Digital Recording, Transmission, and Playback Formats

There are several different standards for transmission of digital audio signals. Each format is, in theory, capable of accurately transferring a binary bit stream. As long as each 1 and 0 is faithfully communicated in its original form, there should be no degradation at all in the signal from one piece of digital equipment to the next. However, if you find yourself in the middle of a room full of experienced audio gurus, you will definitely walk away wondering if any format will ever provide perfect cloning. The validity to each argument for or against AES/EBU, S/P DIF, S/DIF-2, fiber optics, MADI, or any of the proprietary systems lies in the quantification of errors. Cable quality and length also play a role in the accuracy of the digital transfer.

Audio Examples 9 through 13 compare an original source to three different digital copying formats and a straight analog to analog transfer. The examples were recorded first to DAT at 44.1 kHz, then transferred though the specified process. Each example was then transferred digitally into a computer for editing in Digidesign's Pro Tools. The Pro Tools files became the source for digital mastering. The only variable in each chain is the digital transfer process in question. Listen carefully to each example and tally your opinion.

1. Original source (acoustic guitar-oriented)
2. AES/EBU
3. S/P DIF
4. Fiber optics through the ADAT Light Pipe
5. Analog out of DAT A to analog in of DAT B

Audio Example 9
Original Acoustic Guitar

Audio Example 10
AES/EBU

Audio Example 11
S/P DIF

Audio Example 12
Fiber Optics/ADAT Light Pipe

Audio Example 13
DAT Analog Output to DAT Analog Input

AES/EBU

This stereo audio protocol is a professional standard for digital audio transmission between various digital devices. This file transfer format was developed jointly by the Audio Engineering Society (AES) and the European Broadcasting Union (EBU). The two-channel digital signal is transferred through a single high-quality mic cable using XLR connectors. This low-impedance transfer system allows for cable runs of up to about 100 meters with minimal degradation, offering accurate transmission over longer cable runs than the other formats.

S/P DIF

The Sony/Philips Digital Interface (S/P DIF) is often available on professional digital equipment, though it's really the standard for digital transmission between consumer devices. The digital transmission process is similar to AES/EBU but it is not the same, nor is it cross-compatible. S/P DIF format typically uses RCA phono connectors, allowing accurate transmission over much shorter cables than AES/EBU. S/P DIF protocol provides for digital transmission of start ID and program ID numbers, whereas AES/EBU does not.

SDIF-1

One of the pioneer formats in the digital recording industry was the Sony PCM-F1. It used a conventional videotape recorder to store digital audio information, with both channels of the stereo signal multiplexed onto a single video line. The PCM-F1 used the consumer version of Sony's SDIF (Sony Digital Interface Format) protocol. The professional version of the SDIF protocol was used on the Sony PCM-1600 and PCM-1610 converters, typically recording to a 3/4-inch U-Matic professional-format videotape recorder. This combination was the preferred mastering system for years. SDIF and SDIF-1 are the same format. The term SDIF-1 came into use to differentiate the protocol from its successor, SDIF-2.

SDIF-2

Sony's PCM-1630 mastering system updated the SDIF protocol to use separate cables for left and right channels, along with a word clock channel on a third cable, for syncing accurate digital transfers between SDIF-2 systems. SDIF-2 allows for backward compatibility with SDIF-encoded tapes—anything recorded on the older format will play back on the new. This protocol allows for up to 20-bit digital audio. It also includes various control and synchronization bits in each word.

SMDI

The SCSI Musical Digital Interface is used to transfer digital samples between SCSI-equipped samplers and computers. This protocol is up to 300 times faster than a simple MIDI transfer is, and its connections are made with standard SCSI interface cables.

MADI

The MADI (Multichannel Audio Digital Interface) protocol defines the professional standard for the transmission of multichannel digital audio. This transmission scheme is compatible with many professional digital recorders and mixers, allowing for the transmission of up to 56 tracks of full-bandwidth digital audio.

DASH

The DASH (Digital Audio Stationary Head) format is used in high-quality digital multitracks. Sony and Studer offer reel-to-reel multitrack recorders in two-, 24-, and 48-track versions. The multitracks use 1/2-inch tape with provision for either a 44.1- or a 48-kHz sample rate.

Digital Audio File Formats

Most hard-disk-based recorders import multiple types of digital file formats. If the recorder cannot directly import the format, there is typically a conversion option capable of changing nearly any digital audio file to the type preferred by the device.

Sound Designer and Sound Designer II
These are the native file formats used by Digidesign products such as Pro Tools, Session, and Master List CD.

AIFF—Apple's Audio Interchange File Format
AIFF files are preferred by most Macintosh applications. These files can be used in various software applications, but they're best suited to use in the Macintosh environment.

WAV—Windows Audio File Format
The WAV file format is supported by most Windows software applications and many Macintosh applications, though many applications require format conversion to operate optimally.

WAV files are common in the broadcast industry. When sending source material to a computer-driven radio environment, it's common to save 32-kHz WAV files to CD in an ISO 9660 format. These files can be transferred directly to the broadcast environment with no format conversion.

QuickTime

QuickTime is commonly used in multimedia applications. Developed by Apple, this audio format is best when in the multimedia authoring environment, using software such as Adobe Premiere or Macromedia Director.

RealAudio

RealAudio is Progressive Network's format for streaming audio over the Internet. This format allows for various sample and bit rates. Since this is an Internet format, audio quality and accuracy might be sacrificed, depending on the specific application. For example, sometimes an Internet file needs to be quickly downloadable, and audio quality is sacrificed in the interest of file size conservation.

This file format also lets the user determine whether the Internet surfer can download the audio file to his or her computer or to a portable audio file player. On the other hand, users can also prohibit the RealAudio from downloading altogether.

SND Resource

The Apple sound resource file type is supported by some Mac software applications, but it's also commonly used by the Macintosh operating system for alert sounds and other system-specific audio applications.

MP3

This format revolutionized consumer audio mobility. The MPEG-3 compression scheme provides decent-quality audio in a compressed size. These files, by nature of their reduced size and user-selected settings, range in sound quality from pretty good to mighty bad.

Parameter options aim to provide audio in the proper size and configuration for expedited downloading and minimal data storage size, while still allowing the user to intentionally choose increased sonic quality at the expense of decreased speed and increased size. Whereas CD audio uses 30 – 50 megabytes for a typical song (about 11 meg per stereo minute), the MP3 conversion process is capable of scaling the same song to between eight or nine megs and 200 – 300 kilobytes.

This format has changed the manner in which the music business must operate due to the passion music listeners have for swapping their music over the Internet. Artists with major record labels are losing money due to this song piracy. On the other hand, many artists are being heard and are developing huge fan bases because of the quality and inspiration of their music rather than the whim of a record executive.

MP3 is not really a viable professional audio format for music, though it has found use in the arenas of radio and television voice recording due to the less stringent requirements for voice recording and the immediacy and ease of Internet delivery.

DVD-Audio

DVD-Audio format utilizes the same PCM recording process as a traditional compact disc. However, DVD-Audio is much broader in its capabilities. Whereas a CD provides 16-bit, 44.1-k audio resolution, DVD-Audio increases that up to 24-bit, 192 k. DVD also provides much larger storage capacity in addition to six-channel capacity and much faster data transfer speed.

DVD-Audio specifies two different formats (one with video and one without). A regular DVD-Video does not contain DVD-Audio sound specification; however, the hybrid format contains DVD-Audio and DVD-Video, along with a traditional CD layer.

Specification	DVD-Audio	CD
Audio Format	PCM	PCM
Disc Capacity	4.7 GB - Single layer 8.5 GB - Double layer 17 GB - Double-sided dual layer	650 Mb
Channels	Up to six	Two (stereo)
Frequency Response	0 - 96 kHz	5 - 20 kHz
Dynamic Range	144 db	96 db
Sampling Rate - Two channel	44.1, 88.2, 176.4 kHz or 48, 96, 192 kHz	44.1 kHz
Sampling Rate - Multichannel	44.1, 88.2 kHz or 48, 96 kHz	n/a
Sample Size (Quantization)	12, 16, 20, or 24 bits	16 bits
Maximum Data Rate	9.6 Mbps	1.4 Mbps

Super Audio Compact Disc (SACD)
Philips and Sony worked together to develop a more accurate and efficient recording process than the compact disc—the result is the Super Audio Compact Disc.

In recent years, audio professionals have migrated back to the two-track

DVD-Audio Formats and Compatibilities

Format	Contents	Player
DVD-Audio (no video)	Audio disc with optional text, menus & still pictures but no full-motion video	Audio-only, DVD-Audio and Universal players
DVD-Audio (with video)	As DVD-Audio plus DVD-Video	Universal player and DVD-Video player (no DVD-Audio)
DVD-Video	Video with no DVD-Audio content	DVD-Video & Universal player
Hybrid	DVD-Audio (and DVD-Video) plus a CD layer	DVD-Audio (& DVD-Video) & CD players

analog 1/2-inch tape format because of its superior smoothness and sonic accuracy. The SACD format attempts to match or beat the capabilities of previous analog and digital formats, using some existing technologies along with a new approach.

SACD provides frequency response from 0 – 100 kHz with dynamic range greater than 120 dB across the audio band. SACD is often described as musical, detailed, transparent, and with an increased sense of space around each instrument and voice.